Animals of North America

MOUNTAIN LIONS

by Christa C. Hogan

FOCUS READERS

www.northstareditions.com

Produced for North Star Editions by Red Line Editorial.

Photographs ©: Suha Derbent/Shutterstock Images, cover; Sylvie Bouchard/ Shutterstock Images, 4–5; Appfind/iStockphoto, 6; creativex/Shutterstock Images, 9; anankkml/iStockphoto, 10–11; Scott E. Read/Shutterstock Images, 13; Ultrashock/Shutterstock Images, 14, 26 (left); Red Line Editorial, 16–17; critterbiz/Shutterstock Images, 19; Peter Day/The Victor Valley Daily Press/ AP Images, 21; MaZiKab/Shutterstock Images, 22–23, 26 (top), 26 (right); outdoorsman/Shutterstock Images, 25; Eric Isselee/Shutterstock Images, 26 (bottom), 29

ISBN
978-1-63517-036-8 (hardcover)
978-1-63517-092-4 (paperback)
978-1-63517-195-2 (ebook)
978-1-63517-145-7 (hosted ebook)

Library of Congress Control Number: 2016913370

Printed in the United States of America
Mankato, MN
November, 2016

About the Author

Christa C. Hogan writes fiction and nonfiction for kids, teens, and adults. She lives with her husband and three kids in North Carolina.

TABLE OF CONTENTS

CHAPTER 1

CARNIVOROUS CATS

Elk graze in a moonlit valley. A lone shadow prowls nearby in the dry grass. The shadow is a mountain lion. This animal is also called the puma, panther, cougar, and catamount.

Mountain lions hunt at night and twilight, when light is low.

Mountain lions carefully and quietly stalk
while hunting.

The mountain lion studies the elk. It picks out an older, smaller doe. When the doe wanders closer, the mountain lion pounces. It knocks the elk off balance. The mountain lion's powerful jaws tear into the elk's throat. The mountain lion drags its catch back into the cover of long grass to eat.

Mountain lions are **carnivores**. They eat mostly deer and elk. But they will also eat rabbits, turkeys, and even porcupines.

A mountain lion makes an average of 48 kills each year.

Mountain lions are one of the fastest **predators** in North America. But they cannot run long distances. Instead, they stalk their **prey** from the cover of grass or from high on a cliff. Then they pounce on the prey from behind. The mountain lion often breaks the prey's neck with its powerful bite.

 **Mountain lions sometimes pounce
on their prey.**

9

CHAPTER 2

SILENT, SPEEDY PREDATOR

Mountain lions are great hunters. When looking for prey, their eyes can spot motion even in dim light. Their ears move independently to better locate sounds.

Great eyesight helps mountain lions hunt when it is dark.

Mountain lions can reach 8 feet
(2.5 m) in length. Their long spines
make them extra flexible.

Each ear hears sounds from
different directions. Once a
mountain lion finds its prey, it
quietly stalks closer. Its large hind
feet step into the print left by its
front feet. This helps it hunt silently.

Mountain lions rely on their
senses to hunt. They also use

Mountain lions can run at speeds of 50 miles per hour (80 km/h).

strength, speed, and surprise to catch their meals. They can leap 15 feet (4.5 m) into a tree, and they can jump down safely from a height of 60 feet (18 m). This helps them chase, pounce on, and capture prey.

PARTS OF A MOUNTAIN LION

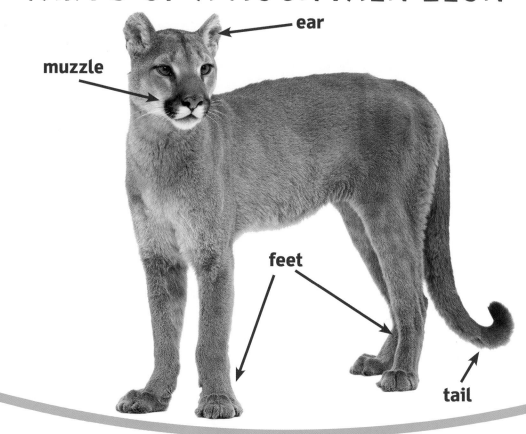

ear

muzzle

feet

tail

Mountain lions are North America's largest **native** cat. They can weigh 80 to 180 pounds (36 to 81 kg). Their long tails help

Mountain lions cannot roar. Instead, they **caterwaul**, chirp, purr, and scream.

them balance. Their tails have black tips. Mountain lions have tan fur with white **muzzles** and bellies. Their colors help them blend in with rocks and dry grass.

Pacific
Ocean

North
America

Atlantic
Ocean

where mountain
lions live

N
W E
S

CHAPTER 3

A CAT OF MANY HABITATS

Despite their name, mountain lions do not only live in **habitats** with mountains. They are found in Canada's forests. They live in Arizona's deserts. They also live in tropical jungles in Mexico.

 Mountain lions also live in parts of South America.

Mountain lions live wherever they can find enough food and cover for stalking their prey.

Mountain lions live alone. A mountain lion's **home range** overlaps with only a few other mountain lions. They urinate in piles of leaves or pine needles. This tells other mountain lions to stay away. They make **dens** in thick undergrowth, caves, or rocky corners. But they rarely stay at a

One way mountain lions mark their home range is by clawing trees.

den for more than a few days unless

they are raising kittens.

GHOST CAT

Many mountain lions' habitats are decreasing in size. Humans are constructing more buildings and taking up more wildlife space. This is especially true in California. As human communities grow, mountain lions are forced to hunt closer to where people live. Mountain lions keep their cover very well and are even sometimes called the ghost cat. But they are much closer to many living areas than people may think. One in particular, named P-22, roams the Hollywood Hills of Los Angeles, California.

A mountain lion sits perched on a power pole in California.

CHAPTER 4

FAMILY LIFE

Even though they live alone, mountain lions seek out one another to mate. This happens in late winter and early spring. Females give birth to one to three kittens every other year.

 When they are approximately 10 days old, kittens open their eyes.

The spotted kittens each weigh less than 1 pound (0.5 kg).

A mother moves her kittens to a new den every few weeks to protect them from predators and male mountain lions. The kittens' spots also provide extra **camouflage**.

FUN FACT

A mother mountain lion will leave young kittens in a safe den while she hunts for food. She then moves her kittens or drags her prey closer to the den.

A mother mountain lion teaches her cubs to stalk and hunt.

MOUNTAIN LION LIFE CYCLE

Kittens are born in the den.

Adult mountain lions are ready to live alone.

Kittens open their eyes and begin to play.

Young mountain lions grow and start to lose their spots.

North American mountain lions live for approximately 10 years.

Soon, the mother teaches her kittens how to hunt. They stay with their mother for two years. Their spots slowly fade away. Then they each leave their mother and find their own homes and mates.

FOCUS ON
MOUNTAIN LIONS

Write your answers on a separate piece of paper.

1. Summarize Chapter 3 of this book. What is the main point of Chapter 3?

2. Why do you think mountain lions have so many other names?

3. Which part of a mountain lion is black?
    A. muzzle
    B. tail
    C. paws

4. What might happen if a mountain lion kitten does not stay with its mother for the first two years of its life?
    A. The kitten might not learn how to hunt prey.
    B. The kitten might not find its own home range.
    C. The kitten might not lose its spots.

5. What does **independently** mean in this book?

    A. working on one's own

    B. working together

    C. working only at night

Their ears move **independently** to better locate sounds. Each ear hears sounds from different directions.

6. What does **stalk** mean in this book?

    A. to hunt and call loudly

    B. to hunt quietly and secretly

    C. to hunt out in the open

Instead, they **stalk** their prey from the cover of grass or from high on a cliff. Then they pounce on the prey from behind.

Answer key on page 32.

GLOSSARY

camouflage
Colors that make an animal difficult to see in the area around it.

carnivores
Flesh-eating animals.

caterwaul
To make a harsh cry.

dens
The homes of wild animals.

habitats
The type of places where plants or animals normally grow or live.

home range
A territory or fixed area containing hunting lands, water sources, dens, and lookouts.

muzzles
Animals' noses and mouths.

native
Living or growing naturally in a particular region.

predators
Animals that kill and eat other animals.

prey
An animal that is hunted and killed by another animal for food.

TO LEARN MORE

BOOKS

Gish, Melissa. *Cougars*. Mankato, MN: Creative Education, 2012.

Person, Stephen. *Cougar: A Cat with Many Names*. New York: Bearport Publishing, 2012.

Riggs, Kate. *Cougars*. Mankato, MN: Creative Education, 2014.

NOTE TO EDUCATORS

Visit **www.focusreaders.com** to find lesson plans, activities, links, and other resources related to this title.

INDEX

C
camouflage, 24
colors, 15

D
dens, 18–19, 24, 26

E
ears, 11, 12
eyes, 11, 26

H
habitats, 17, 20
home range, 18

J
jaws, 7

K
kittens, 19, 23–24, 26, 27

M
mating, 23

P
pounce, 7, 8, 13
predators, 8, 24
prey, 8, 11, 12, 13, 18, 24

S
spots, 24, 26, 27

Answer Key: 1. Answers will vary; 2. Answers will vary; 3. B; 4. A; 5. A; 6. B